Lightning Rhymes

Navin Manik

ISBN: 978-87-973519-0-1

You & I can't be defined even if we try just like this Universe
The third eye that shines the divine is the energy purely magical
The signs we sight in this life are the intuitions supernatural
The scars that I wire in my I is to revive the deeper connections
The rhymes that I write in line are the lightning of my raw interior

To learn more about Navin & his work, visit:

Website   : navinspoetry.com
Instagram   : @navinspoetry_

A Poetry Collection:

A Poetry Collection:

Speechless I Became

Speechless I became
When I saw the glimpse of me
Felt a sudden shift
Paused were the thoughts
Everything came to a halt
Tears began to fall
Soul wanted to scream
Inner pain was so real
Wounds wanted to heal
I began to breathe
Transparent in the moment
Vulnerability at its peak
The moment of inner peace
Where joy and sadness were one
Good and bad had no meaning
Darkness was the Light
Loved that very Sight
The moment of true Presence
Where Heart was the only Sense
Truth was the One
When I saw Me

It all started here when I felt the very first time this need to express my state of Being in the form of this poem

When You Look Into Me

You looked at me
With those intense eyes
You smiled at me
With those beautiful lips
You cried with me
With tears in your eyes
You held me tight
With those earthly arms
You gave me space
With that loving heart
You were there for me
With those meaningful words
The impression of you
Is permanent in me

The energy from the moment
Has struck me deep
The sole purpose of you
Was to look deeper into me
Where Pain & Agony
Were the different forms of Love
Where Spirituality was the only Reality
Where there was space for Anxiety
Where things were as they are
Where Manipulation was very far
I am no one
But the reflection of you
I see myself in you
When you look into me

Lightning Rhymes

Living in thoughts could be comfortable
Embracing the present seems unacceptable
Reality can be so unbelievable
Pain-body is snapping me to unusual
Loving edges of perfect imperfections
Healing the soul is sole intention

Deep scars on my brutal blood surface
Arrows piercing in my broken top shelf
Bleeding river from my sensitive vessels
Crying ocean when I'm feeling restless
Feeling crazy when I skip the deep breaths
Unleashing devil when I'm manic anxious

Extinguishing sparks to calm the burning ashes
Expressing emotions to hit the freaking reset
Grinding patterns with my mindful presence
Writing lines with my wondered senses
Lightning rhymes with my thunder pencil
Riding waves in search of peaceful balance

Crystal Green

This is the real feeling in my heart that I wish to share & write about coz it's living in me

I'm projecting the scene of my vivid thoughts that I play & then I pause on my pitch black screen

These days I paint the inside of my walls with the color of your soul, you're all over me

Your light penetrate my dark even when the sky is lit with moon & stars, you're the shining beam

We're a thousand miles apart but I can feel you by my side, it's just not some dream

Your divine energy is simply pure, it's intense & burning hot, you're magical & serene

You're my heavenly waterfall, you remain holy even when you fall, you're rounding my edges & healing me

You're kissing my every ounce, even though I'm full of deep scars, you're the spiritual being

You're the melody to my song, I wanna hold you in my arms, you're my beauty & I'm your beast

I just want to say it loud that I love you with all my heart, you're so beautiful crystal green

A Dot of Hope

I'm just a dot if you zoom out to see the spot on this beautiful &
lively zone

That's all you want if you wish to lock when you hold the shaft &
look patiently through the scope

I'll turn into thick fog if you take a shot with your tainted thoughts
painted with senseless strokes

You dreamt that I would rot when you put the mark at my heart
from the other side of the shore

You better check your clock coz I'm on your watch to put a stop
on your timeless goal

I know you wish & want but you simply can't block coz I'm
simply a free & formless soul

It's the way I talk whether you like it or not but I'll free you from
the twisted knots crippling your very core

I promise I won't haunt from the very top to crop your vulnerable
& shielded ghost

Coz I've walked on the path full of thorns & my drops that looked
like the bed of roses

So I'll simply take you to the dark to show you the burning sparks
from daunting dot of beautiful hope

Achieve

Am I here to achieve a few things?
You see, if I put my heart & bleed
I can reach heights with ease
I might feel a bit dizzy & weak
But I won't change to deceased
But is that what I really need?
Sometimes this all sounds like some disease
Do you get what I really mean & seek?

I know we all are human beings
Hungry to fulfill our different needs
But it makes me to wonder & think
Why do we run over our own kind to get that seat?
Why do we scream at each other & create a crazy scene?
Is the purpose of our lives to simply fight & compete?

Sometimes we do nothing but to preach
Sometimes we create confusion with such a great speed
Sometimes we infuse panic & chaos, which lead to stampede
Sometimes we want to hide the wrong doings & not to be seen
Are we a part of hunger game & ready to kill our own breed?

The current way of doings & achieving is quite obsolete
I'm just projecting this picture that I've been sensing
Just try to listen & consider a few things
I'm simply suggesting, I'm not here to teach
Real joy comes from the heart & its beat
Simply let go the air that we tend to breathe

All I want is to sow a few seeds before I leave
The holy water will do its own magical tricks
The seeds will then turn into the magical trees
We are all different creatures with a common means
The essence of this thing lies in the very being
So let's spread the love that's necessary to live

It's time to bring awareness while we walk on our own feet
That ripple in water can be sensed from the seven seas
Let's open the gates of our hearts to the real & loving deeds
Let's open the mind's eyes to redefine what an achievement
should be
Shallow life with labels is unstoppable calamity
Sacred path to infinity is pure spirituality

A Kiss from The Devil

Whisper kiss of yours
On my lips is crazy
You're the devil
Sitting next to me
Covered in pure beauty
You're so sharp & curvy
Curving the formless at me
Confronting the demons in me

Panic is summoned
Anxiety is entering
I'm now willing
To kiss your evil
To breathe you in me
Your eyes are burning
Your hunger is thirsty
Your teeth are feasting

My flesh is beasted
The blood is streaming
It's all so dirty
My neck is tainted
The floor is painted
Your hold has tightened
But I'm not frightened
You are so enchanting

The impression of you
Tattooed on my neck
Deep pain is agony
I want you desperately
To pain me tremendously

To draw your devil on me
With the red ink I bleed
Ecstasy is creeping

Enlightened by your devil
Tormented from head to toe
Fragmented is my peace
This picture is so lively
But if you can't sense it
Then it's insanely deadly
I'm loving every moment
A kiss from the devil

Beautiful Soul

You are the beautiful soul, the being & the core of my life
You are the beautiful creature, who disappear when I close my
naked eyes
You are the true blessing, asking me to look beyond the hue & cry
You are the greatest teacher, spreading wisdom to live & not to die
You are the master, that showed me the I in you & the zen of
daunting sky

Sensitive, sensible, sweet, strong & so intense
If the things aren't the way you intend
You get too high & often very tensed
You feel all alone & your world becomes too dense
I can sense the fire inside you when you're close to lose your
dance
All I want is to be with you so you can find peace in my presence
Hold you tight in my arms & connect with you at the deeper level
I'll walk with you on that string in search of the fine balance
You are my sun - the intense verse of the U.N.I.verse

The Demons In Me

The demons in me
Are screaming and dancing
Making me restless

The demons in me
Are whispering and laughing
Making me nervous

The demons in me
Are twisting and turning
Not letting me breathe

The demons in me
Are nesting inside me
Trying to break me in pieces

The demons in me
Are a part of me now
So I let them stay without giving attention

The demons in me
Are simply Reflections
My own Interpretations

The demons in me
Are Control, Ego and Pain-body
Nobody but me can set them free

The demons in me
Wish to open my Heart
So I let my Self leave & be the very Being

Am I The Only One?

Am I the only one feeling like this?
Am I the only one shredding in pieces?
Am I the only one screaming through verses?

What's happening to me that I'm tearing?
What's hitting me so hard that I'm breaking?
What's giving me this numbness that I'm shaking?

Why am I looking in dark with empty eyes?
Why are my lips sealed & throat so dry?
Why am I feeling like fire, that's about to die?

How can I survive when the light is fading with time?
How can I walk when my track is disappearing into broken lines?
How can I breathe when the air is suffocating my silence?

I'm shivering the shimmers with pure tremors
I'm twisting the beautiful minds with my terror
I'm traumatizing the hearts with my demons

My temple is screeching, I see the cracks in my brick
My heart is lonely, I stand at the brink of my flips
My soul is bleeding, I inhale the ashes covered in my red ink

Automatic

It's simply automatic & kinda symptomatic when I'm out to see the unsystematic flow of this inner darkness when I layer myself with the transparent sheet that looks quite fantastic coz it's ornamented with the fragments of my provocative thoughts

But the sword on my claustrophobic plot is dancing so hot as if it's about to sore & cut open my throat to penetrate the screaming walls of my cracked fort that in reality can't even afford the heavy blows coz then it throws the red pearls out to the shore to shut down the light of my burning core

This whole coat the unseen holes on my shaky course with the pragmatic approach to integrate the scorching arithmetic quotes by simply torching floors filled with scouting horrors with the glow of a rhythmic unknown to simply show the unmatched power of the so called smoking soul

But then this cinematic scene explodes & I freely fall on this ecstatic floor where I start transcribing my countless flaws with my crazy traumatic claws into the poetic form where I take an accelerated pause to finally get lost in the edges of my sleepless jaws to wait for another daunting but quite exotic dawn

Your Eyes

I can see in your beautiful, big & deep eyes
How you're feeling, your eyes can never lie
I can sense the restlessness in you & the whole is crying
The deep ocean is red-blue-green & is crazily sighing

Every teardrop is creating symmetrical ripples
Your ocean is sending waves to the heaven
The nature of your heavenly body is pure & heathen
Just like the universe in its own beautiful way is healing

You don't need to say a single word, you must know
Your eyes are dripping every word, they know every bit of you
The desire to dive deep to reach your bottom, before I hit the very
shore
To catch my breath, to meet your divine & to see your beautiful
core

The Real Meal

It's like when I write my lines & describe a few things
I'm just grinding to tell how it feels when my mood swings
By crushing the stones into rough & fine powder that I mix
With liquid to make this soothing & so therapeutic paste
To heal the mental bleeding, wounds & physical pain

I tend to set my scope to fire my own head in flames
Take myself & my surroundings down with my anxiety that I face
This moment I paint no mercy to pain the sensitive scene of the
rusted shield
I come out suddenly from my dark, broken & isolated shed
People see me changing my form into this evil with eyes burning
pure red

And then it seems as if I'm about to freak out the freak in me
A bloodthirsty sinner in those sparkling & scary scenes
Everything around me turn into ashes with my scorching heat
And it seems as if I feed my mind with my dear ones sufferings
But I get deafened by the chains of my own crazy & loud screams

I can't hear when they constantly beg me in fear to stop while
they're in tears
But no excuses, coz it's explicitly me, who's exhibiting the evil in
me
I only wish to unchain myself in reality, to get freedom from me
So I end up wandering in search of the balanced recipe for my
crazy craving
Manifesting inner peace – the definition of the real meal & by that,
I mean real me

15

The Slate

Staring at this empty slate
Want to scribble my current state
But heart isn't ready
Mind is talking crazy
Simply can't breathe
And on top, I'm about to scream
Want to break that screen
Why do I feel so aggressive?
Or am I simply just possessive?
But I know am worked up & explosive

This noise in my head
Want me to seriously shed
The ray of blood shade
But it ain't make no sense
So I try to take a nap
But thoughts make me react
The role I then enact
The throbbing in my chest
As if I'm on this unending chase
Don't know where it would take
I feel my life is on stake
My whole body starts to shake
Grass is full of deadly snakes

But is it all in my head?
My mind is playing brain dead
So I take the knife in my hand
To cut away this deep pain
In hope to truly retain
The things I lost back then
But what would I really gain?

It's not like I had the holy grail
Would I still give a damn?
To build that shattered old dam

It's not really a simple game
When you ain't snipers aim
You've been living in shallow fame
The stories you surely did tell
I'll erase it one day from your slate
You see our talents are innate
But I don't believe in checkmate
It's not the way I want to relate
It all makes me question & think
While my eyes stop to blink
What's the point of bonds & links?
Am I imprisoned in me with those chains?
Why my world seems to shrink?

But then I see a little lively bird
Flying high in clear sky with no dirt
It lives in now & with no hurt
The pain disappears with a single sigh
The deeper calling to fly high
The eyes deep ocean in true joy
The feeling is beautiful & so divine
The sun has been shining very bright
I think I've got it somewhat right
The pure moment without that knife
The pieces of puzzle, I mean this life
The mountains, I feel I can climb
You see, this ain't just a rhyme
It's a story of my inner fight
But now it's time to clean my slate
And go to bed before it gets too late

Darkness and Light

Darkness and Light
Are they states of mind?
Light in Darkness
Darkness in Light
Is it so black & white?

Diving in the Darkness
In the womb of Mother Earth
To find the safe haven
To die and rebirth
Where formless is the very Form
And timeless is the only Time
Darkness in Light
What a pure delight

Amidst Thunder and Storm
Where the dark Skies roar
The inner Volcano is about to explode
The blaze of Lightning
Penetrates deep in the Heart
To burn the Light
To show the true Path

The power, the beauty, the wildness
It is the crazy dance of Light & Darkness

Questioning

Is everything changing?
Tweaking
Is the mind chattering?
Freaking
Is the body shattering?
Exploding
Is the rhyme flowing?
Phrasing
Is the rhythm beating?
Creeping
Is the ink bleeding?
Deadly
Is the color red beets?
Dead beats
Is that beast feasting?
The Red Feast
Is the heartbeat racing?
Panicking
Is the air fading?
Fainting
Is the screen getting blurry?
Sweating
Am I afraid in reality?
Suffocating
Has the time stopped moving?
Lonely
Have I started reaching places?
Phases
Am I going crazy?
Frenzy

Do you get what's happening?
Suffering
Can you sense the feeling?
Burning
Are you here to catch me?
Destiny
Are you one of those preachers?
Creatures
Do you come from the shadows?
Lightning
Is this all a part of me?
Questioning

My Barrel

So you think I'm looking daggers?
Would boil everything till it vapors
Then you didn't get it right
It was never about the fight

If I did not fire it out
It would've burnt me inside out
Now don't even try to get me wrong
I didn't fire to burn them down

But if you want me to pretend
Everything is simply perfect ten
Then let's live the fake lives
Live the lie & put on the smiles

So should I now start to think?
Before the paper gets my ink
But then it won't be the same
I don't believe in prefab frame

If I can't see myself in my eyes
What's the point of sun & sky?
That stone in the ocean is an average five
But it still lives its purest life

Why to live the life from the shallow?
When the bones are full of marrow
You see, life is everything but narrow
Here I am spreading the ink from my barrel

Oh Dear Rejection

Oh dear rejection
Who are you?
Are you a feeling?
Or an emotion?
Do you have a purpose?
Or some worthy reason?
Are you my weakness?
Or truly my strength?
Are you a teacher?
Or may be a preacher?
Do you even exist?
Are you an illusion?

Everything happens
Happens for a reason
So many questions
Coz you are my creation
You are the pain
Hiding for so long
You are the one
The painful Heart-opener
Oh dear rejection
I know you well
You are the love
Dressed in another form

Darkness – The Intense Light

You see, darkness ain't just black if you see it right
It's truly divine & that beautiful deeper sight
It's that blessing on me, which makes me stand upright
From there I see the things, that aren't just shallow & fine

The shadows & reflections have their beauty, right?
The sun sets in the west to welcome the dreamy night
The beauty of stars & moon from earth, courtesy darker skies
The lightning hit the ground when the clouds roar & cry

Would you lit the light if things were always bright?
Darkness is just another shade of the inner light
Be that thing that breathes & shines the life
Darkness is that intense light, that's living inside

My Mind

Let me give you a ride
And take you inside to this site
To give you some insight
Into the arena of my simple mind

It's been a while since I found sleep by my side
It's just this one little thing with me
Too many thoughts are nesting inside
Questioning me day & night, the meaning of life

I feel like detonating my thoughts
To simply blow up my own mind
To make some space during the sleepless nights
To change those formless kinds into this form of rhymes

My mind phrases these words & scatter them on this dark page
Just like the shining stars sprinkled all over the dark space
The constellation of burning stars you see far far away
Where the unknown finally meets its ace, the card of spades

Your Presence

Right in this moment, I'm craving for you – Crazy for you
I wish to kiss your soft lips – Flow of passion
The desire to bite you – In pure ecstasy
I won't be able to keep my hands away from your body – The
curvy forms
Just want to dive into you blindly – A beautiful moment
The dream to melt & disappear in you – The magical universe

But it was time to open my eyes from the subconscious
You weren't here with me in your physical form
I felt though your pure energy from the sacred zone
It's beating heavenly & hot
I feel your presence close to me
Pure intensity in a single shot

No, it wasn't my longing – I felt your touch
It was so tender & deep
No, it wasn't the moment of desperation – I smelled your scent
It was so fragrant & toxic
No, it wasn't my anxiety – I heard myself screaming your name
It was so real & yet surreal

You are the tide of my heart
You are the love that truly shines
You are the loving beat so divine
You are the hypnotizing dance of serpentine
You are the sensual glance of valentine
Just wish to show you this crazy reality before I die

Set Me Free

The glimpse of you
Refreshed the memory
The sense of you
Close to me
The presence of you
Is pure intensity
The voice of yours
Is sitting in me
Every word of yours
Is roaring inside of me
Takes me back
Makes me sad
It makes me cry
I am losing control
Is the glimpse of me
Being left alone
Is the presence of me
No hand to hold
Are the words of mine
Let them flow
Free the soul
Free the mind
Wish to set you free
Let me BE
Set me free
Just set me free

The Silence

I can hear the silence
Silence is violent
Violence is fighting
This fight is painful
Pain is so hungry
Hunger is craving
This craving is crazy
Crazy are emotions
Emotion is a feeling
Feeling is deluded
Delusions are explosive
Explosions are hurting
Hurt is not worthy
Worth is so dirty
Dirt is though earthly
Earth is the grounding
Grounded in deep gravity
Gravity is levitating
Levitate the outer space
Space is full of circles
Circle of tiny dots
Dots are the elements
Elements are flowing
The flow of pure smoke
Smoke is formless
Forming the eternal soul
Soul is the purest beat
Beating of heart
Heart is breathing
Breath of inner peace
Peace is to love

Loving to live
Living to keep dying
Dying to relive from the deep

My Halloween

I feel this crazy need
To tell & simply scream
It's not that I'm mean
And I don't want to demean
But it seems like a theme
No, it's not halloween

I've been trying to win the fight
Against this force that holds me tight
It makes me lose the clear sight
When I can't see the burning light
As if I'm entangled in the dark night
No, it's not the scary & secluded site

I hear & it seems
Something is living deep in me
The way I'm breathing
As if I'm stuck inside of me
The air is not flowing freely
No, I'm not feeling pity & crying

And if that wasn't enough
The turf is now quite rough
All I want is to punch it so tough
And to hit it with a spinning curve
To break open the skies to tears
No, it's not about being fierce

The only way is to look deeper
The only moment is neither past nor future
The only I is the eye of wisdom
The only truth is the eternal love
The only God is this Universe
So I take off my hood to reveal who I am

Grasp Rings

So you decided to block scene
After you discussed & talked things
I know you felt my writing
You meant, it wasn't the right thing
But you didn't play the right strings
I know you don't like my rhyming
Coz I like to reveal the hidings

Honestly, it didn't shock me
To sense how your mind thinks
But it would never stop me
To jot when I realize things
I really don't mind this
Coz I don't ever write themes
To like me or to like them

There is never a time-line
To read those fine lines
It's never about the limelight
I talk about the life size
That people ought to sideline
Which is not some sci-fi
You see, I don't believe in sigh-fight

Sense what's your I size
Just don't rely alone on your eyesight
Coz it's all about our heartbeats
But only if you can grasp rings
When a drop hits, the O(cean) sings
When a heart opens, the whole syncs
Mind isn't always the bright zing
Start connecting with your kind Being

The Edge

I sit sharp on the edge of my bench in the dark with a hatchet in my hand to break open my senses & to claim that my pain in the veins is not vain but insane

But I get so mad & a bit sad when I spread metal scraps on myself coz then I bleed the beads so discreet on my crease to decrease the misery

So I feel quite shaky as if my skin is so thin like a leaf & it starts to burn instantly to create the debris that comes out from the heat of the seed

I'm torn at my core that I feel this need to ease & burn my peace into pieces on the street that's filled with so many deep & some holes unseen

So I scream in infinity with my fluctuating beat coz I can't simply breathe & it seems I'm the beast hinged to the scene of the shattered dream

I relapse on my screen coz this all feel so diseased when I see this degree of release & then I step explicitly into the bed of fire to become the deceased

But then I focus on to drop my sores with the source of my scope in this hope that one day I'll for sure end this whole to simply blow everything to the pure

Crystal Clear

The moment I met you
I felt something special
Just didn't know what it was
But now it's crystal clear

You're the heavenly drop of rain on me
You're the scintillating light that's healing me
You're the sparkling star that's burning in me
You're the beating heart that's living in me

The depth of your fine lines
The rhythm of your deep rhymes
The imagery of your heartfelt writings
The expressions are so mesmerizing

The grace in your face paradise
The shine in your crystal green eyes
The melody of your angelic voice
The beauty of yours is pure divine

When I think of you, I smile
When I miss you, I sigh
When I long for you, I cry
When I see a glimpse of you, I die

I see you everywhere
So I kiss you in air
And I whisper your name
Sounds crazy? Yeah that I am
Coz I am deeply in love with you, my dear

Pure

It's dark outside right now in the scene of cold winter
The heat is on but my longing for you makes me to shiver
So I hold a corner of my pillow as if you're with me under the
layer
And I kiss your lips passionately & then whisper that I love you

I'm burning my senses with your fire, you're simply so irresistible
I'm digging my ground deeper, you're the depth unreachable
I'm filling my page with your essence, you're the line of my every
verse
I'm seeing beyond my deep scars, you're the light of my universe

My face is glowing with your aura when I look into the mirror
My eyes are sparkling with your crystals, it's pure love that I river
My heart is beating with pure joy, your healing is simply magical
You're the smoke of my soul, you look quite hot & so spiritual

Loneliness

It's late at night as usual & my mind is on wandering spree
I'm very sleepy at present but sleeping is not my first priority
Spears are slowly piercing in my head, they're paining me
constantly
I'm hearing a loud knock on my door, oh it's just my spiraling
anxiety

I'm holding the edge of my bed
Coz I don't want to let loose & scream
So I stare in darkness with my scarred phase
When I sense the river of my salty tears

I can't take it, I'm breaking
I can't brake it, I'm shaking
I can't make it, I'm falling
I'm losing my senses & it's driving me crazy

I'm sinking in deep hole as if I'm slowly disappearing
So I start to talk things out as if I'm freestyling
And I jot my feeling down to give the effect of rhyming
But deep down I long for a pure touch, my heart is simply crying

Loving & Living

The flow of blood, that's streaming
The flow of air, that's breathing
The percussions of heart, that's beating
The thoughts of someone, that feeling

Butterflies
Connecting
Dancing
Dreaming
Healing
Shining
Singing
Smiling
LOVING

But then the lightning struck in its own beautiful form
The shields are up to protect & push away the loved ones
Everything changes instantly to welcome pure sorrow
The lungs inflate & deflate heavily & it feels so hollow

Crying
Emptiness
Longing
Missing
Restless
Tearing
Thinking
Sadness
LIVING

It feels like the heart is burning in the ice cold furnace
Phrasing phase to face requires enormous courage
But this crazy love won't disappear from the core & its blood
surface
Love is the heart of this beautiful, light & dark universe

My Poetry

If the things were only up to me
And my vault were stashed with greenery
I would exit the world of perfect geometry
To enter the universe with heart fueled poetry

I'm in love with scribbling the meaningful schemes
It's my way of expressing how I truly feel
The lyrics synchronize with frequency of my heartbeat
The percussion & vibration of the immaculate beast

Now let me stitch the pieces a bit differently
Just stay for a while, hear another thing from me
I share my stories with the same original intensity
You see, this is my healing process & my own therapy

I know it's kinda provocative the way I project my themes
It doesn't matter what you think of it & what you think of me
It's not gloomy to throw light on the darker scenes
You see, the darkness is so light can be

My rhymes are self-realization & experiences with deeper meaning
It's my way to explore the burning fire & the formless being
This is how I see the things now & this all was meant to be
My poetry is the flow in me & it's the soul I simply set free

Complicating the Simplicity

When I sit on my hot seat to see the lively scenes on my fractured screen with absolutely no screams, everything seems seamlessly lovely & spotless from the safe distance of those crazy complexities

Just let me be & let me breathe and let me see, if you can really see through when I project my transparency of the transparent me through the window, that transpires the red ink into the frame of moist & mixed feelings

You see, it's not possible to understand a single word if the divinity of this world won't be unfolded coz the understated unknown energies are being underrated & underestimated by the human nature, that's simply busy in blowing the overrated & meaningless smoking swirls, generated by some useless extrapolation of quite simple assumptions, which in turn takes the mankind to the senseless & rusted junctions

So many different meanings of a pretty simple thing is just like demonizing the simplicity & degrading the cold feeling after the aftermath of burning flames, when it's very much possible to sense the unseen but still, one keeps throwing the senseless theories without actually smelling the essence of pure simplicity & acknowledging the power of the unseen energies

It's senseless if you try to make sense of every single word separately, but if you simply sense the flow of pure energy, you'll see a whole deeper dimension of this crazy scribbling

So do you get now the complexity of simply complicating the simplicity of simply me?

Trip-Track

Ripping the new tracks for my upcoming trip
Burning are the numbers with crazy deep lyrics
Upbeat to find the intense on this trip so scenic
Unseen is the route, where the unknown bleeds like a civil

Looking closely into my baggage to check what to upkeep
Unkeen to bring the new & to lose a few old things
The new is asking me to embrace but I'm hesitant to see & let it
stay
The old is hiding with a different face but I ain't desperate to find
& let it phase

Excited to explore but anxiety is tricking me
Wondering if the heart will remain inside of me
Speculating if I'll find peace when my rest would be in pieces
Questioning if I'll rip my heart out, would my soul then R.I.P.?

The necessary I must absorb & digest on the way of waves
And the rest must pass through me without any claims
The tracks will for sure burn my body consciously
To leave my naked marks as the permanent prints eventually

Surrender, Acceptance, Faith, Existence are the treasures in my
S.A.F.E. of open space
What You Believe Is What You See is the reality I believe &
resonate
It's a trip filled with mindful & mindless tracks that I walk while I
levitate
The tracks on this trip that I play are the forms of my life that I
live & meditate

Bleeding Numbers

Losing my grip & feeling numb is quite a rubbery feeling in my
flesh
Speeding in ambulance at the speed of light as I lose my stance
Noisy sirens chasing the streets as if I'm becoming so discreet in
those lanes
Bleeding inside of brain is so draining and is pure insane

CT & MR scanning show the big spots & some huge round clots
Paralysis in left arm, hand & left side of face, simply can't
comprehend
Not able to lift my arm is quite noticeable challenge
Epileptic cramps on the left side of face & arm as they are
harming my brain

But I'm not about to lose without giving myself a chance to
withstand
I'll wrestle back my arm to let loose the heavens, the storm if I can
I must find my inner peace & my inner calm to fallback
Family, friends & job matter the most – that's the ultimate
strength
I'll fight back to finally come back from the horrors of the graves
This is a my promise, I won't rest – it's dawn of fire, it's my roar

Freeing my Soul

Clicking my jaws
Flipping my flaws
Painting my falls
Skipping my pulse
Breaking my calm
Screaming my raw
Caging my thoughts
Snapping my bars
Forming my sword
Slitting my form
Revealing my scars
Bleeding my drops
Paining my dark
Chaining my dawn
Burying my ground
Burning my whole
Freeing my soul

Sacred Connection

It's a story of this unique kind
Naked spirit & so divine
Full of energy, a playful type
A real handful at certain times
Not afraid of jumping from the higher skies
This sensitive soul is registering the crazy noise
Is the purest blessing in innocent disguise
Love the passion in the beautiful big eyes
Expresses the joy & pain in major size

A new colorful day begins
Under the shining blue stars
The intense fire is burning
In deep space with black holes & scars
Striding towards big world in smaller shoes so cute
Mesmerized by depictions of fiction as if it's all so true

Irresistible
Sensible

Let me be me are the heartfelt screams
Orbiting all alone sounds like a scary dream
Visuals are heavier on that delicate little screen
Emotions are throwing curves on the swirling scene

Start now to connect the first alphabet of every single line
Sacred connection you'll discover, it's just not a simple rhyme

Heavy Eclipse

Things are getting kinda heavy in the now
I feel, I'm drowning deep underground
Want to disappear before I turn into a blood thirsty hound
To catch my breath without that heavy echoing sound
And to find the inner peace where I can be found

My world seems plain & a bit insane these days
Perhaps it's my eyes covered in the shadow haze
My favorite colour blue is turning into this gloomy shade
Burning all my energy but still can't keep up the pace
I want to believe it's all unreal & it's just a phase

You see, the small green is eclipsing the infinite pink
The thoughts are on the brink of the insanity & suffering
The mind draws me to this dungeon, where demon is the king
And words are written on its rough surface with my dark red ink
The pain-body appears so fresh even though its condition is not
mint

May be I'm simply just dreaming
Or may be this has a deeper meaning
Where I find myself wandering the unending scene
Where the Gods too have the darker side or so it seems
And the Demons on the other hand, aren't all that mean

This place where I've reached is slowly emptying
Where the screen in my head stops blinking
It brings me back to the surface & stops me from sinking
The heavy eclipse disappears to reveal the heart that's beating
It's the moment where everything melts down to simply nothing

Drop-Dead

Zipping my lips softly after sipping my warm cup of coffee
Closing my eyes gently to feel the different energies in my body
Smelling the scents mindfully to find the right sense of spirituality

Following my instinct while I walk on my ground with thoughts
bare naked
Surrendering to the surroundings full of doubtful dots & broken
bridges
Letting myself to let loose different shades on the surface of rusty
edges

I keep on rising up to raise my bars to unlock myself from my
mindless self
I fall freely on the heavy grounds as if I'm trapped inside those
tiny droplets
I feel like a raindrop that gives life when it bursts & dissolves in
the soil, it's simply drop-dead

Smoking Sacred

I don't know how to tell you this
But you're in my every single script
I hope you can feel when you read it
And I hope you can see how I see it

You entered with your blue heaven in my dark sky
You looked with your green crystals in my brown eyes
You poured your pure love in my wounded life
You shined your golden light on my blinded side

When I walk in fresh air, I breathe your verses
When I bathe in hot water, I steam your presence
When I look in the mirror, I reflect your crystals
When I touch my chest, I hear your music

We're over a thousand miles apart, our energies are strongly
bonded
My heart is filled with your love, there are no empty spaces
I'm picturing you & me together, our bodies are purely naked
We're melting into each other, the souls are smoking sacred

Fluctuations

Everything in the beginning seems so fine
No complaints whatsoever, they're hard to find
Then you tell me, I'm the reason that you're happy

Your life is now a pretty ten
Everything is clickin' & making sense
It's the life you've been dreamin'
The perfect picture ready to be framed in

But you see, time has its own perfect sign
It keeps moving on without a single sigh
So now you tell me, I'm the reason of your suffering

Your life is now pretty tensed
Things are crazy broken & make no sense
It's the life you don't wanna live at all
Broken & sharp mirror all over your ground

But tell me, are you just presenting me in your virtual reality?
When it has nothing to do with virtue & reality
I can't be the reason of your contentment & casualty
And I won't take the credit or the blame of your reality

Finding peace amidst storms & being restless in serenity
Are the fluctuations of your inner scene
When your very being is the only thing
Unaffected by the nature's countless blinks

Have you noticed the black screen in your brain?
When your thoughts stop talking & you don't need to strain
It's that state where everything simply standstill
It's the moment of endless love, inner peace & real zeal

You're this very Being, observing from your third eye
You're the caravan of this life that never truly dies
Where to live is to constantly die
Was the talk between the Self & the I

The T-Tour

Throttling the twisted thoughts
Trespassing the traumatic top
Trekking through the thirsty throat
Tear-dropping these teasing thorns
Tearing the toughened turf
Throwing the tainted timid throne

Thrusting through the tangible tangent
Trusting the tremendously tranced treasures
Thriving these timeless twinkling therapies
Treating the tactless tender trees
Thickening this to transcendental transparent thin
Thanking the true transpiring transformation thing

You are The One

Stop hiding from me
Stop running away
You are the one
You are the only one

You are crystal clear
When I close my eyes
Stay with me
Don't disappear

The imperfections in you
Are simply perfect
The way it is
Is the only way

The delicate rawness you possess
Takes my breath away
You are The Consciousness
You are that Very Being

White Angel

Once upon a time I was sleeping in my bed
The floor started to shake when two dark energies entered, it's
quite bad
They started pushing me out with power & their black magic spell
I was quite weak in my legs, so I couldn't defend myself
But then I saw a white angel held me with her bare hands
She used her pure energy to throw the dark energies out of my
deck
The floor stopped shaking after those evil energies were swept
The white angel sat beside me as she was completely drained
The power she used to save me was enormously grand
When I looked at the white angel, my eyes were at a constant gaze
The godly angel was wearing the delicate white dress
Her big eyes were simply radiant & her beauty was immaculate
This white angel with pure energy was the savior of my space
All I wanted to do was to close eyes & kiss her beautiful lips
I fell in love with her the very moment I met her being

The Shed

I was about to drop dead on my bed
But then I took a walk into my shed
That led to this fine old thread
I used back then to sew the cuts when I bled
I did slit my finger with the razor sharp blade
To self-check, if my blood was still thick & very red

My path seemed so blurry in those photo-chromic specs
I had sleepless nights & then those crazy headaches
I felt as if I were sometimes spitting fire & some lead
You won't understand what was going on in my 20s brain
There were times when I was completely drained
And on top, those frequent rides in the slow moving trains

Unsure what I wanted to do with so much stuff in my bag
Heavy burden on my shoulders & on those two skinny legs
But how would you ever catch up if you never lagged?
Coz there were times when my life was in jet lag phase
This is just not a phrase as I was really afraid
I would look in the mirror & ask who's that unknown face

It's OK if you judge me because I don't give a damn
Hiding isn't my thing coz I'm so very real
Crazy drills & soul searching is my recipe to sustain
I am just a normal man, who's vein gets sometimes jammed
Open your mind & heart and perhaps then you would understand
It's not just me but everyone has that sort of shady place
The only way to come out is to go deep inside your very own
crazy shed

Many Frustrations & Manifestation

It's like punching with my own hands my own spiralling journal
Feeling as if the ink is becoming thicker & so infernal
Adding one extra sickness due to this sickening kernel
Loosing sometimes my mind, though the soul is eternal

Brain hemorrhage has been raised with epilepsy in this game of revelation
The medicine I take, is quite heavy in the current prescription
The feeling that I'm doped, isn't some mindless imagination
My head is heavier with these crazy thoughts due to shear exhaustion

Shaken & shocked to the core after this new information
I didn't realize till now, I could've been ashes, my true confession
I thought back then, all I needed was a few weeks of rehabilitation
This all is dragging me down to new levels of frustration

But I'm still dedicated to move in the true direction
Motivated to balance my imperfect feet to perfection
Ready to work harder to get back the grip & sensation
Steering wheels through this bumpy ride to reach my stable station

It's all about healing in real time without maximum acceleration
Perhaps this all has a deeper meaning, it's beyond sense perception
It's to heal body & soul with therapies, mindfulness & meditation
A new chance to reignite my life, the beginning of my own manifestation

Unstable Ground

So hear me out
What I'm about to jot
Aren't just my random thoughts
This is what I experience coz
I'm sometimes simply so stressed out

It's not so simple to deal
When I change myself into the beast
Who's feasting on other's meat
The blood on the floor that I spill
But then I wipe the floors out to crystal clean
To hide the pain & suffering to unreal

Whenever I open my big mouth
And say a few things a bit loud
The misunderstandings I then create without a doubt
Coz I lose my mind so fast & then I freak out
No patience in me, I can't breathe the air at all
So I spit fire on others to burn myself down

The desire to break the walls to take my frustration out
I lose my control & then I explode with that deep sound
To burn everything into ashes with my fiery spark
And cover the clear sky with the thick fog

I know this isn't my real face, it'll be phased out
It's crazy tough, that's what I've been screaming out loud
This all is sitting in me deep, so I'm isolating from this thick crowd
Coz I know I'll find the balance on this shaky & unstable ground

This Very Time

The scene changes at this very time
When darkness surrounds my every sigh
My mind then starts to whip a cry
Is this the beginning of another sleepless night?

I want to flame my burning thoughts
And I wish to tear those greyish clouds
To reveal the moon full of darker spots
Was everything a dream or just a fog?

The shadowcast on my inner wall
The silhouette of my naked scars
The intensity of my dreamy eyes
Why didn't I see the blinking lights?

The demons are crawling like tiny spiders
The surface is bleeding with shiny diamonds
The heart is beating with noisy sirens
Have I started losing my edgy grounding?

Arrows are piercing through my lyrical mind
They're hitting me hard & smashing my silence
I'm drowning in these waves of the lows & highs
Is that why I'm screaming these crazy rhymes?

The learning of this beautiful life
To accept the unexpected with open lines
I let loose myself to be that kind
Am I smoking into the deadly sign?

The Twin Flames

Once upon a time
He saw this woman so beautiful & divine
She was the goddess with intense eyes
Her dance was sensual & mesmerizing
She was wearing red, her moves were hypnotizing

She was dancing bare feet on the sandy ground
Splashing waves was the music in the background
The campfire lit the scene in the dark
Her face was radiant in those golden sparks

His eyes were fixed on this beautiful divine
He was watching her closely with view bird's eye
He was drawn to her immensely, no surprise
She wanted his attention, no denying
She had waited for him long for several lives

He landed close to her, as if he had the wings to fly
They looked deep into each other's big & passionate eyes
Instant love & connection, the two sacred hearts
He flew back to his place where he belonged
While he was carrying her in his arms

He was an Egyptian king in his past life
She became his queen, the one with the title of his wife
She was the only one, who could see through his eyes
She filled his life with a purpose, her love & pure divine
The twin flames still burning, they're one of a kind
The magic is still living from the flames of their past life

Poisonous

You're wearing this bloody sensual body suit
Your seductive eyes are big & beautiful ocean blue
Every step you take is calculated & very shrewd
You're holding me tight in your tender arms of unbreakable loop

You're dragging me out of my castle of haunted moods
My face is hidden under the layer of my shady & torn hood
You unhide my crown of thorns with fire of your intense look
Those piercing thorns in my head are painful but I'm keeping my cool

A single kiss from the sensual & poisonous lips of yours
Makes me bleed red diamonds, while I bloom into the scene so blue
The scars on my face look scary in this surreal reality so brute
I can feel I'll soon be running on fumes & will for sure be doomed

I spin 360 degrees to see the swirling point of view
Your bite will slowly dissolve my flesh & bones before I forever snooze
This cruel nature of yours is so seductive & very crude
This whole picture is so dark while I'm hanging on this edgy hook

This very moment I dig my ground deeper to find my roots
I only see those huge shadows in the shade of gloom
I don't need to speak loud or write down to show you the proof
Everytime I come closer, you disappear in air with a single poof

I'm searching myself desperately inside of you
Ecstatic rush in my blood when I taste the poison in you
I'm so much in love with this poison & poisonous you
I'm flying high in my smoking to be forever with you

Sharpening my Edges

Turning up the volume while I dance carelessly just like the tipsy
being to caress the restless eternity
Shaking my wavy long hair just like the silverbeast I breathe to free
the freak in me
Twisting my body just like the scaly serpentine to sway swiftly in
this slippery scene
Sensing the delusional beliefs just like the demons I breed inside
of me to burn my inner skin
Fighting relentlessly just like the fluctuating flame that lit my dark
nights with shadows of anxiety

Cutting the silence with the violence of my violet violin that's
snapping the tightened strings
Ripping the dead layers of my poisoned cells to fill the dark spaces
with light full of raw intensity
Carving my rough face with my senseless fingers to project the
formless edges of my blinded insanity
Filling my fountain pen with thick red to sketch my mountain of
rocky emotions to draw sensitivity
Sharpening my edges on rough surface dipped in salty water to
tear the fear through the visuals of my poetry

My Words

It's getting late in this chilling cold night
So I'm trying to close my very tired eyes
The problem is that they aren't at all dry
My thoughts are galloping but I don't know how to ride
My fingers are frozen, so I'm struggling to freely write
But here I am still awake to simply freestyle

I'm just expressing how a trainwreck feels like
I could be brain dead but I'm very much alive
Honesty is what I breathe & not the lies
The highs & the lows of this crazy life
Everything seems unreal in pure real time
My walls were once painted with pure real joy

I won't give up easily coz I love you so high
Until I hear one last time, it's all over & goodbye
Coz I can still sense the pure energy deep inside
I know you love me, it's just not in my mind
The beautiful crystals so sacred & divine
The melodious voice so sweet & so fine

My words are forming this formless fire
My heart is braking, it used to freely fly
I guess, I wasn't the type even though I did say & type
I'm lost & shaking, there's no inner light
I'm blue & shrinking but I still see your shine
I feel like bagging myself to forever hide

Surreal

You see, it all appears so real
And yet the things are quite surreal
I don't even know what I'm doing here
I can't resist it, I'm about to shear
While I breathe this dark & heavy air
Perhaps I write this all to simply share
To root my thoughts to an absolute nowhere
To simply explore what's going on up in here
I think, I'm just trying to clear the unclear

Perhaps these words aren't making any sense
It's not about the logic, just be very present
They are in tenses & quite a bit intense
Feel the cold heat & smell the odourless essence
You see, these words are simply effervescent
They disappear before you can even comprehend
It's my way to rebuild my old & broken tent
By tent, I mean the very existence of my own presence

Eyeing My Phase

The heart is eyeing my phase while I am crying
The air in my body is heavy the way I am sighing
The mind of mine is red diamond when I am mining

The fire is burning my track that I trace on thin icing
The demons are scratching my face while they're dancing
My feet are losing the balance, so I'm simply sliding

Time is chasing the zones that once were hiding
The walls of this form are cracking & now they're falling
I'm unchaining my case that was suppressing the deeper calling

My voice is whispering to burning stars as they keep shining
The soul is grounding my whole in soil as if I am dying
This all is enlightening the core, it's so exciting

The Free Flow

The anatomy of my soul is smoked in ashes with bold & if I try to extract the pure essence, then my whole will only hold the unwanted dark holes

You see the highs & the lows are the waves that splash & roar in rows in search of the very unknown in an open space that's yet to be explored

So I keep healing my inner sores that are still bleeding the very core to steel breathing my mystical form so I steep soaring in the infinity zone

I am the free flow that see through my deep soul & then I tiptoe in my being mode to free me from my beast mode to seek peace & bring the sweet hope

You & I

I'm flying high in the clear blue sky
My eyes are fixed on you with pure desire
Your sensual curvy form is making me to sigh
You look burning hot with your intense fire

The beauty in the beautiful you, it's pure divine
The beating of your beautiful heart, your love is making me to dive-in
The beautiful fragrant essence you spread, I'm deeply in trance
The beautiful silhouette of you on my surface, I'm simply entrapped

You are the magical scenery, I'm the dark shade on your canvas
You are the infinite universe, I'm the black spot in your shining space
You are the vast ocean, I'm the sharp edge in your deepness
You are looking at me in the mirror, I'm the tear sitting on your eyelid

This Animal Is Back

Don't walk like this in your silky skin in front of me
Incredible
My craving for you is crawling up a mountain frenzy
Irresistible
You're looking red hot & my eyes are burning destiny
Inflammable

Gaining your trust while I throw you with my raw strength on turf
Animal
Messing with your mind & body while I pull your messy hair
Animal
Tearing your peace in pieces while I look deep into your big eyes
Animal

Whispering my twisted words in your ears to reach your red crystal
Sensitive
Sketching on you with my sharp nails to make you whisper pain
with your deep vocals
Sensual
Shaking you intensely to awaken your senses to make a connection
with your crying soul
Spectacle

Biting your tender flesh slowly to calm my hunger with my hungry
teeth
Oh, I feel like an animal
My lips are sticky & shaded as I taste the thick red that you're
bleeding
I think, I'm an animal
Even the wind under dark heavens of hell is howling crazy
Yeah, I'm an animal

I see you in my mirror & my lens is bleeding red visuals
Ahh, I'm so bloodthirsty animal
I see you in my shadow & I look like that fiery dragon
Wo, I'm so scary & brutal animal
I see you shattered on my ground & then I disappear in darkness
to be one with the new you
Yeah, I am that tainted & untamed animal

R.E.A.D.

Refining
Evolving
Accepting
Defining

Reforming
Evaporating
Absorbing
Dissolving

Responding
Exploring
Allowing
Deciding

Revolving
Exploding
Alarming
Declining

Unmask

I often find myself caught
In the middle of my thoughts
When I sit in the dark
I then take heavy shots
At my cage full of spots

When I stare at burning stars
It feels as if I'm a frozen dot
I'm restless on my ground
The tears then I freely drop
From the eyes of my heart

The waves & the shocks
The flash & the sparks
I rise then I fall
My flesh bleeds when I walk
The pain speaks to me loud

The chains cut my song
The layers I then rip apart
The patterns hit me hard
The disc cracks & it parts
The track trips my path

I scratch scars with my claw
My demons in me freely crawl
I'm hungry but I simply starve
So I scream & then I roar
I'm this wild animal so raw

I'm imperfect full of flaws
My ink leaks as I jot
My poetry isn't just the art
It's my life that I prompt
It's my soul that I unmask

Standing Upright

I hear they are scared of me
Afraid to approach & talk to me
First they put that blame on me
Then they try to take a hit on me

They fear I'm that crazy volcano
Ready to destroy their yappity yap canoe
Burn the waters they're sailing on
Coz I'm the intense fall of the Canyon

Unwilling to cooperate
They tell me I just operate
Simply deny to solve what they point at
With no copy or roger that

I heard so many allegations
They ran me down with accusations
I lost for a moment the sensation
So I ended up in total confusion

They wanted me to find the solution
I needed to be fixed was the conclusion
There was a huge interference in the discussion
So I left the things in shock & desperation

That night was gloomy & dark
The kick in the guts was deep & hard
It kept me awake in my thoughts
Replaying that scene was painful & odd

That scene brought me back to the senses
And then I went out for a walk in my 10's
I kept asking myself the hows & the whys
My voice was heavy when I looked up at the skies

But to give up at this stage, wasn't in my mind
My dear ones were there for me & stood by my side
The facts in my head, I started to write
To make them realize that hit wasn't alright
So here I still stand tall & upright

Burning The Soul

Curves on my scene
Writing on the screen

Spots in my brain
Mending the frame

Numbness in arm
Playing the b-ball

Sweat on my forehead
Focusing like insane

Restless is my mind
Resting to thrive

Snapping the strings
Isolating in my crib

Losing my skin
Feeling so sick

Death in my voice
Tearing ocean to dive

Burning the soul
Stomping the floor

Staring at stars
Sensing the void

Closing my eyes
Balancing the path

Beasting the art
Beats of my heart

The Devil's Face

The desire to rip off the devilish face
Pump the blood out of the bloody arteries & veins
Need to burn the body in intense fire & flames
Slice the remains in sharp pieces & small scales
Cut the bones with saw, the sharp rotating chain
Everything collapses, no screams & there's no pain
Cook the flesh in thick blood till it's tender & changes its shade
Finding the demons that reside in haunted & crumbled shed
Hiding behind the intense & provocative lens
Made of complex geometries with that improperly proper base
This scene looks so scary from your narrow & twisted lane
There's a fine line between your sane & my insane
Feel the heat, I'm not here to dig your grave
The gory imagination is an art of this devil, the creative brain
Just show the true you, that's living behind your face

Reflections

It's all started coming back to me
It's like watching a movie on tele
This tv is nothing but my heart you see
It's sending the pictures of you & me

The Hero, The Comedian & The Villain you seem
Sitting on the surface of thin skin you wear
They push the buttons to make you feel
The one that you think you wish to be

But is it that reality you want to breathe?
The Good, The Bad, The Ugly is so cheesy
The role of your existence is way milky
The ground you stand on is not shaky

Now rewind all over to watch it again
Give full attention & just do not scan
Dig a bit deeper under that sensitive skin
This time you'll notice how it all began

Wear the glasses to see that extra dimension
The God, The Love & The Being we mention
The brightest star of the heavy production
The DNA of this magical creation
Is all within you beyond sense perception
Close your eyes & sense the deepest relation
Finding yourself is self-realization
It's you & me and our sacred reflections

Healing Soul

Thoughts were racing in my head
Surrounded by misunderstandings coz I was so afraid
The pain looked like that cool stitches on my brow
Snapping on near & dear ones with that insane flow
Loosing my head as if I were about to sink & permanently drown
Blinded by ego as if I were that king wearing the diamond crown

I was crushing everyone into pieces to make place for myself
How could I be so self-centered by being eccentric?
How could I be so cool & calm by being frantic?
At times my mind was crumbling to fine dust
My demons were shutting me down with deep cuts
I was trying to run away from myself on a paper-thin crust

I was living half alive, blinded by this all
I'm listening to your enchanting & sweet songs
I'm learning to stand on my feet when I fail & fall
You're healing me spiritually, you're healing the sores
I'm spreading my wings slowly to raise my spirits to soar
You live in me, you live deep within my core
I'm so close to you coz you're my divine soul

Inner Music

What does music mean to me?
What's the rhythm & melody?
What's the meaning of its lyrics?
What's the depth & its beauty?

It's like when the blood in my veins is playing the riffs
When the heart of mine is thundering drum beats
When the eyes of mine are blinking the high hat
When the mind of mine is compiling the different sounds

Silence is the lyrics that I write for this unique song
Deep voice I possess to sing my own lyrics
It's blowing the self away & melting down the lead in me
It's pushing me beyond my untested & untrusted limits

Light & Darkness I use on my sound stage & screen
Connecting with my inner audience, which was once forgotten
behind my scene
I'm lost in this divine music that unites me with the energy of the
unseen
This is the salient sound of my inner music

Transparent

The sky paints this transparent scene
The clouds are floating freely
The sun rays pass through the beams
The nature of magical energies

The airwaves sync the melody
The highs & lows flow exquisitely
The ripples are echoing the sea
The ground is rooting my feet

The track is ripping my skin
The layers are burning to thin
The time is watching it still
The drops are cleansing the film

The naked is pure not obscene
The change is to unchain the theme
The patterns are revealing the unseen
The scars are opening the deep

The seam is melting cracked piece
The noise is filtered to peace
The voice I break is to feel
The rhymes I ride is to be

Images

I am a ticking bomb but I don't want to really snap
This ground is shaking, it's just me not the quake
I look like a solid rock but I'm crashing down to simply crack

The countless spots in my scan, are like bullets fired at close range
This image is burned into my head, where I'm shooting with my
rage
I'm trying to find my peace but it's hiding behind those
transparent layers

When I stare at my ribcage, I see a broken heart & a broken face
If only I could cut open my chest to let loose my inner pain
I'm screaming loud in closed space so my heart can finally escape

I see these images up in my head where I'm lying down on my bed
Publishing my last lines on social media & texting goodbye to my
friends
Talking one last time to my family while my soul is about to
ascend

I'm not afraid of death & honestly, I haven't given up on my
myself
I'm just enraged coz I can't always fit the pieces of my broken
frame
So I get engaged with my demons to char them into burning
flames

I'm losing balance on my tricky track, so I pause to take a deep
breath
To simply sense my manic phase, it feels as if I'm breaking into
shaky flakes
One day the fire will penetrate in me & change everything into
smoke & ash

Mindless Brain

The drops in veins
Are the thoughts insane
The talk in vain
Is to prompt the phase
The song I sang
I drop the face
The sign that rays
The darkest day
It's time to race
And write the date
To account the rate
Of the countless deaths
Of the tiny cells
That reside in shades
Of the mindless brain

The doubts are bad
Are like dots embedded
On a darker shed
That's propped with paints
But honestly
It's to pop the pain
On a block with pen
So I strike the pins
To disembark the bane
I rock the string
To shock the wave
And I shot the blame
To fog a name
That's bothering
The inside of me

The sky is red
And the ground is rain
I lost the track
So I walk the lane
To find the peace
I define the pace
I blind the drapes
To light the sense
I side the rage
To sight the sage
And I spine the strength
To eye the main
I fine the thread
And dissolve the ends
To finally embroid the change

Longing

Picturing you laying by my side
While we hold each other so tight
The smell of your hair & skin
Draws me even closer to you with a blink
The tender touch on your pretty face
Makes you smile with that haiz
The deep ocean in your beautiful eyes
The sacred connection of our beating hearts
The souls are doing most of the talk
But I know your voice is sweet & warm
The bodies start burning immensely hot
When I gently kiss the soft lips of yours
The sensual feeling to move & dance
When you put me into the loving trance

The way you breathe in that very moment
Truly spiritual at a deeper level
You lay your head gently on my chest
And we drift away in the mysterious mist
The universe stands still in total awe
When our bodies melt together into one
You are so close to me in sense perception
And yet so far away from a different dimension
The longing to be with you is not some crazy dream
If I cut open my chest, you'll see how I bleed red tears
You're a blessing with a formless form
That I cherish from dusk till dawn

Blinking Ph(r)ase

Staring at the blinking cursor on this dark page
Feel the need to sprinkle brilliant dark dust from my scarred phrase
Even in darkness, I can see the reflection of my manic face
But it's my perception, coz this is just a frantic phase

Situations
Correlations
Aggression
Restlessness
Elevation
Desperation

Nerves are controlling me from time to time
That's what you've been reading in some of my rhymes
Thoughts have started knocking the door of my mind
Asking me questions imprinted on my wrecked slides

So many questions are shooting in my head
But I can't find the answers, not just yet
So I decide to take the small steps to feel safe
To see the impressions on my path that I walk with respect

But then I sense my real senses
That bring me out of the situations in my verses
That has been throwing curves, a few of them reversing
It's the real life scene with zero rehearsals

Where my pain-body vanishes just like the ghost from this page
It brings my pieces back to the real & peaceful state
Where my form remains formless & perfectly imperfect
Where my scared state changes into the sacred space

Colour Red

I'm standing outside in my garden
Looking up towards the sky & the clouds
I hear then a roaring sound
The lightning hits & shakes my ground

The sky is crying just over my head
I feel the droplets are hitting my entire self
But then I notice my ground is changing its appearance
My whole body & ground is muddy & looking so crazy dense

I raise my head towards the sky in the space
The passing clouds are flying like death
The sky looks so different in this bloody shade
Just like this bleeding in my crazy head

Everything has turned into this colour red
But then I feel a gentle touch on my hair
It's treating my wounds with love & care
The healing effect has begun, I can truly sense

Patterns & Forms

Thoughts are hovering over me & words are difficult to express
this
It's about the inner struggle, so don't look at outer appearances
I'm witnessing turbulence in windpipe of my crazy experiences
Spearfishing in deep ocean to catch the reflection covered with
mist

Trident in my body from a distance seems like a bloody cool
piercing
The peers are now facing fierce battle & everything is bleeding
Change is what I'm these days observing & it's just not some crazy
feeling
Change isn't that easy if you're afraid of sharp chain of pain &
suffering

Old patterns struggle as they've started losing their insane control
They try hard to disturb the peace of mind as they intensely scold
& troll
They fire cold forms at me to push me back into the deeper hole
It's a battle between the old & the new and I'm about to explode
to explore

It's not a dream....surely
Surely, I'm burning inside out
I'm in fear....purely
Purely, I'm sensing the vibrations so loud
Change is creeping in me....slowly
Slowly, it's striking from cloud to ground
Seeing it now in me....closely
Closely, I'm engaging with my new form

Freestyle Roar

My sky is shifty & I'm speeding on my floating cloud
Inhale this air & exhale my lungs out
Shatter windows to break open my crazy house
Stand on my reckless ground than to be a part of the senseless
crowd
I'm wearing the dark shades & ready to slit anything with my
freestyle roar

I'm losing my balance & my brain is twisting spirals
The blood vessels are about to explode the shiny diamonds
The demon in me is going viral & spitting burning fire
I'm about to hit the rocks with my ice cold desire
Hide yourself instantly to avoid the consequences dire

You see, my skin ain't so thick, so I won't take it with ease
Just don't try to pinch my surface, I'll then play you like a twig
Stop clicking my clicks, if you don't wish me to come after you
with my fits
Stop throwing those bricks coz I'll then crush every single one into
debris
It seems I'm feeling sick & crazy, but I'm simply trying to look for
the inner peace

Reload

The restlessness in me at this moment is dancing
Just like the flame of a candle when you light it
Where panic seems a beautiful lover of anxiety
My phase is pure darkness & it's making this scene so freakin'
exciting

Sidelining my eyes from the memories when you said I was lying
And then you started questioning my integrity while you were
shouting
But your narrow barrel of paranoia was shooting bullets at me,
they were flying
While I kept myself unshielded with honesty & was loving you, I
was still trying

If I'm sitting today in silence & my eyes are wet by crying
It doesn't mean I'm feeling weak & simply hiding or R.I.P., like
dying
Coz the thoughts in my head are bleeding river while I'm
freestyling
And honestly, they seem to be quite shaken in color red & a bit
violent

So I decide to reload my beast mode to free flow my sleek sword
To meet you through your meatloaf & see through your lean
throat
And to reach you & your sweet soul and lift you with a steep slope
To beat things to seek core & walk away in peace while I scream
hope

My Hissssing Eye

I'm so twisted when I lay down in my pit
When things grow crazy, I shed my deadly skin
I look so drop dead when I wear this new suit of scales
My hissssing eyes are wide open while you look at me in fear

Don't gaze at me with that glare, you're just making me insane
Just pray for your life coz you're about to be my next prey
You simply can't escape when I follow your shaky steps
Don't look back at me in despair while I sway my swinging swag

My moves are so swift when I zig-zag & spit at you in air
I'll show you the blues when I bite you, I swear
Everything will change in that moment to the living hell
I'll give you fits before you finally rest on your ground plain dead

Deep & Dark dip

Thinking of those thoughts that thwarted the sense
Started to look deep into those dark pages with my lens
Noticed the tiny creepers were crawling like snakes
Dissolving simply everything with their poisonous kisses

Spawning beautiful forms in fire in pure frenzy
Spinning around the unknown with high intensity
Spearing that dark shadow to red & crazy
Scribbling those words down in bold & apostrophe

Amidst these KOs of chaos & cry
That shadow movement brought me to the deeper joy
The beautiful moment of soul leaving body to fly
The eternal heart connection under the darker sky

That dark page changed in a second its color
It's full of expressions & some grounded flavor
From there I see the dark has its own shimmer
It's the edge of the deep, it'll cut the shallow into slivers

Intense Feelings

It's not a thought in my head, that's what I've been living
You're so real, divine & intense, my heart is simply melting
You're whispering in my ears, your voice is pure magic

Your eyes are deep & vast ocean, I'm falling in them & sinking
Your lips are beautiful & soft, I'm loving the constant kissing
Your touches are wild & sensual, you're driving me quite crazy

You're with me spiritually, our souls are simply smoking
You're the calmness deep within, it's purely meditative
It's not the end of this connection, it's the new beginning

Keywords

Crazy I am
Anger I had
Aggressive I sound
Calmness I embrace
Reflections I see
Shadows I have
Darkness I sense
Fluctuations I face
Phases I phrase
Rhymes I bleed
Intensity I air
Truth I care
Confrontations I dare
Heart I share
Upright I stand

Openness you lock
People you block
Eyes you close
Heart you hide
Shield you wear
Defense you choose
Stories you tell
Words you misinterpret
Lines you delete
Reality you deny
Essence you miss
Self you see
Mind you talk
Time to change
It's never too late

Tears In Your Eyes

Tears in your eyes
Are not your weakness
But the power you have
To melt a stone cold heart

Tears in your eyes
Are the reflections
Of the pure connection
In that blissful moment

Tears in your eyes
Are not just the emotions
But the openness you possess
The unconditional love you are

That tear in your eye
Says more than words
You could ever speak
To express how you feel

Tears in your eyes
Are more than tears in your eyes
They are the vast ocean of love
That flow through your beautiful eyes

Healing My Hell

Sick, sick, sick
I'm feeling crazy in my head from time to time
Sink, sink, sink
The mind is simply mental to hit the lower mantle
Stiff, stiff, stiff
Is my face & the arm on the left side
Sit, sit, sit
When I sweat & lose the balance while my vision gets blurry

Tick, tick, tick
Is the subtle ticking sound of my wounded brain
Sip, sip, sip
All I wish is to drink & dance away my anxiety
Stuck, stuck, stuck
But this crazy epi-lapse-see makes me to cry & scream
Snap, snap, snap
I'm ready to explode & eat everyone alive with my rage

Beast, beast, beast
The second I start swearing & tossing things in air
Beat, beat, beat
The heart is racing with the speed of light
Heavy, heavy, heavy
Is my phase when I feel the piercing thorns in my head
Heat, heat, heat
My blood is burning lava on my swirling street

Lift, lift, lift
I keep falling down & rising up to face my reality
Deal, deal, deal
I hit my brakes to handle the things very slowly
Breathe, breathe, breathe
I close my mind to see the sea of mindful sinking
Heal, heal, heal
Is the only way to live my life away from my hell

The Deep Ocean

I see you so clear
Your sense is so real
The flow in the veins
It all feels so intense
Looking at the sky
Shaken to the very core
The beats fluctuate
The ground resonates
Listening to its tiny voice
Giving attention and warmth
Accepting it whatever it is
Irrespective of its form
Feeling weak and little broken
Wearing bare skin without layers
I am no one but an explorer
Searching myself in the deep ocean

Colorful Theme

I'm trying to close my sleepy eyes so I can finally fall asleep
And I'm covering myself in layers before I impatiently start to
freeze
But my anxiety is propping me to fall hard on my once operated
knees
So I end up playing in dark this reckless game of hide & scream

Can you see my lids are carrying these bloody tears?
Can you feel my blood is boiling in my crazy heat?
Can you believe I sometimes feel like torching my entire scene?
Can you even reach if I decide to bury my body down infinite feet?

But then I dive into your green sea to see me with pure clarity
I play your crystal clear music to string me with sweet melody
I absorb your fine lines to levitate me with this magical imagery
I write the verse of love when I sense your profound energy

I see the moon is shining with open mentality
I see the stars are burning in azure spirituality
I see the sky is evolving with colorful theme
I see the sun is beaming hope inside of me

This all reset the entire picture of my entangled reality
Love is stitching & healing my scars in peace & prosperity
I know, I'm not leaving yet coz I've just come out of catastrophe
You're my sacred mirror, I can see the white light inside of me

Just Heart It

The mind is what a mind is
It twists you & then you cry this
You look away & then you blame it
It's not you, what your mind did
So many excuses to simply hide it
Can you find it, what your mind did?
The fact is you would never find it
Coz everything you do, you confine it
You put the disguise & then you deny it
It tricks you coz you are blinded

In the run to find what your mind did
You keep forgetting you've a heartbeat
Let me tell you what a heart is
Please don't mind it & just try this
Put your heart in to simply find it
This way you would simplify it
The passion in you is pure heart filled
The love you feel when your heart sings
To sense the light your pure heart is
Just Heart it but don't always Mind it

That Man

He's an average man with his own imbalances
He's standing with a lance tipped with steel in his hand
Who pokes other's feelings unintentionally so they bleed coz he's
somewhat scared
The balloons then start exploding with sudden release of the air

Sometimes he realizes too late, then he gets kinda stressed & very
upset
He then wishes to set himself on fire to feel their pain
And to leave his own head, to see himself burning in those flames
To let go of his soul up in the deeper & dark space

Sometimes a single moment can trigger a shot in his head
That everything becomes meaningless & then he becomes so sad
Breathing heavily while anxiety is slowly reaching his door steps
Feeling helpless, so he locks his head with heavy chains to feel safe

He's trying to find his real ground to come out of the
underground hell
He's not trying to be perfect coz he knows no one ever can
But he's trying hard to do everything to be a better man
He doesn't believes in hiding, so he reveals that I'm that man

Shattered

I'm unlocking my phone & checking my post every second minute
But no new mails anymore, there are only empty spaces
I'm feeling cold & my core is burning in agony beyond any limits

It's still difficult to believe, how the things have ended in a split
second
Energies were glowing like the beautiful stars, everything was
smoking sacred
But memories are all that's left behind, the feeling of being one is
burning ashes

My eyes are fixed on a mirror, they look pretty dead & quite rigid
I'm seeing reflections of crystal green but that mirror is now
cracking
I'm touching the cracks on its surface but it's me that's shattered
into pieces

Reflection Hologram

These days my best friend is reflection
But there's no deflection from the sense perception
Simply sensing the vibrations from several different creations
And finding peace in the middle of heavy explosions
Being conscious is what it takes to loose the cautions
This isn't some cinematic fiction, it's just an observation
It's the pure affection with that unknown relation
Where there are no diversions & no manipulation
This reflection takes me to the greater depths beyond imagination

It seems as if this world has tremendously changed
Changed is the scene when I walk outside in the heavy rain
Perhaps my reality has built another picture frame
Perhaps the meaning of life for me isn't the same
Perhaps I see the deeper dimensions projected on my screen
Perhaps I see my reflection in everyone I look at, a thought insane
Perhaps I relate to the pain of every single face that passes by my lane
This picture is so intense than the trillion stars in the outer space
Reflection is what I'm reflecting, it's the hologram of my inner space

Cry

It's been raining heavily every single day & night
I'm breathing ashes, the air is exploding flaming dynamite
The universe seems pitch dark, there's no sign of intense light
I'm drowning in deep sorrow, pain is what I feel & write

I'm sitting still in shock, surrounded by speechless noise
My body is covered in layers but my state is frozen to cubicle ice
My heart is beating with crazy screams of my saddened voice
I don't know what else to do when all I do is to simply cry

My big brown eyes were once shining with beautiful green crystals
so divine
Now they're soaked in sparkling tears, red eyes are all that's left
behind
I dreamt, I could fly high with my broken wings in beautiful blue
skies
But my feet are sinking slowly on heavy ground every moment
that passes by

I'm trying hard to accept & breathe without the painful sighs of
life
The knife is stuck in the I, it won't let me live & it won't let me die
So I close my eyes to sense the deep emotions that are suffocating
my mind
But then I cry even more coz it feels as if I'm witnessing my own
demise

"A" poem

Eyes wet
Mind heavy
Can't breathe
Throat choked
Senses numbed
Fluctuating beats

Speechless as I speak
Reflections I truly see
Crystals are still green
Staring at those scenes
Memories on my screen
The heart simply bleeds

The voice of yours is stuck in me
The lines you used to write to me
The song that you did sing for me
The picture is burnt deep inside of me
The finger twitches as I type in anxiety
The silence fills the air through my poetry

Stuck

Stuck in the deep
Deeply sad times
Time is running so fast
Faster than thoughts in the head
Heading to hit the wall in full speed
Speedy recovery is what we say
Saying things will be alright
All are shaken to the core
Core is losing the hope
Hoping for the best

Gates chained
Chasing the lanes
Raising the dams
Damning the senses
Facing the phases
Crawling like ants
Breathless no air
Shouting for help
Praying like insane
Catastrophe we live

Failing to play
Falling like preys
Reds in the rain
Blaming the heaven
Firing the flames
Burning the dead
Ashes are left
Smoke prevails
Soul lives
Energy is left

Dream

Dream
I sleep in my shed with no sheet on my shape to reveal myself in
this naked dream
Skin
I could sense your delicate presence and your gentle touch on my
rough & wounded skin
Lips
The wet taste of tenderness was breathless when your
reminiscence kissed my thirsty lips
Sync
The beauty & the beast I could reel with the tip of my screams in
one single & effortless sync
Beat
These days my heart is burning in fire & dark memories, so I pen
my art with sighs & I drop the beat
Tears
Longing to belong & to be can stream the rivery of my inner scene
into the whispers of my lonely tears
Green
The thing is that I can see the serene smile instantly & sea the
shine of your waterfall with crystals green
Miss
The pink thread & pinpricks did stitch mess & paint sick but the
fact remains it's still you that I purely miss
You
It's you I mirror & it's you I loved with pure intention but today
only your reflection is left in the song – it's you

Teardrops

The song is throbbing my inside
And the heart is beating the loud sounds
The moon is hiding in dark sky
As the clouds are acting like greyhounds
The memories are causing red sprites
To light my darkish grey ground
So I sit silently at late night
To embrace the moment with teardrops

My Serene Kingdom

Wilting under the tilted splinters
Blinking to see flickering clickers
Playing with my sneaky demons
Voicing my cadence with slippery fingers

Creating this path in deadly trackers
Breaking the norms in small fragments
Braking with claws on warm ashes
Picturing the forms with my naked senses

Scanning the heart in pure silence
Spiraling the sky with mindful timings
Spotting the clouds with sharp lightning
Sounding the dark with beautiful thundering

Shining in my eyes when I glimpse a mirror
Signing these lines to refine the present
Sighing this rhyme when I sea the wisdom
Resighting this site to build my serene kingdom

Painting this Picture

Tear my eyes to ocean
Tear my body into pieces

Break open the dark skies
Break me into phases

Paint my face in thick red
Paint my phrase to crazy

Pain me till I feel the edges
Pain me to find the inner space

Falling to feel strong wind
Falling to reach my grounding

Diving to kill the kill-zone
Diving to meet the unknown

Dying to repair the top shelf
Dying to reborn my whole self

Reflection of A-Mirror

You've left behind a permanent mark in my whole
I know it'll always remain smoking sacred & pure
I hope you can see the light in your crystal clear core

You're more than A-mirror, a magical reflection of the highest
source
You're the breathtaking sparkling waterfall that freely flows
You're the crystal green, the beautiful light that intensely glows

This body suit is just an appearance, a closed piece of cloth
And love is much more bigger than the feeling of "mi amor"
This life is the meditative voyage on waves of the highs & the lows

The only way you would know that my body is ashes in the human
form
Is when I'll disappear from the pages just like the mysterious black
hole
No footprints of mine you'll ever find coz I'm the fine sand on the
shore

I'm understanding the meaning of pure touch that I once craved
for
My gratitude to you for being with me from the other side of this
globe
The Universe is echoing "It's You", just say no more beautiful
soul

Wish

I used to wish this & wish that most of my life
I used to pray to God to fulfill those wishes with my closed eyes
I even sat back with empty hands & regretted this life
But one thing I was forgetting all this time
I tended to overlook what I already had by my side
I was missing the present & was concentrating on the noise
So I started to indulge in steep talks with fluctuations of my
heart

It's here I realized I was all the way so crazy wrong
Coz I started to see the intense sparks on my path so dark
I then switched to live from the deep in the now
I can see the shining light in between countless dark spots
I can sense my wish is fulfilled as I've reached to the sharp point
I finally know the real meaning of the falls & the rise
Just like the immense beauty & power of waterfalls & sunrise

Reliving

I'm reliving tonight the old story
New details but absolutely no flooring
My scene isn't sharp coz it's very blurry
Looking downstairs is difficult, it's pretty scary
Struggling with balance, so I walk very slowly
Small explosions in my head are kinda crazy
So I pack my things while I'm so thirsty
Coz I've called the number & I'm almost ready

My face is stiff like skintight denim
Ambulance is on its way, it's soon comin'
Paramedics popping questions & I'm up summing
Suffocated behind mask but I'm still breathing
No energy in me, I just wanna slip in
Ambulance is reaching hospital's drive-in
Thoughts are running while I'm buckled & resting
Am I on my way to get another bleeding?

Firing Shots

I'm ready to play this crazy game
Firing shots at my mindless brain
Killing the dead spots from point-blank range
Freaking my beast out & the senseless rage
It's time to transform the savage to a sage
It's time to free my soul from this solid cage
I'm taking the steps to change my deeper state
I'm dissolving the imbalance & my wavy pain
These bullets were pointing at my shaky phase
It's to awaken my senses, not to kill me dead

Fluid Lines

The empty space that purely shines
The clouds vaporize the deeper sky
The heart is Universe's loving child
The beats are airing the blazing fire

No game to play by rolling the dice
No armour-sword to protect & slice
No story to hold coz there's no point
No blame or guilt can pain my I

The now is glowing the simple signs
Truth & raw are my intense lights
Black & white is my intuitive choice
The falls are to weather the inside

The golden symbol I've just put aside
The white ring I then carefully eye
The nothingness I wear is dragon size
The path dissolves this very time

The silence in my breathing windpipe
The heat of this frozen thick ice
The drops form my poetic fluid lines
The flow rivers my transparent rhyme

Dying once again to reset my life
The new state is staging the wise
The freedom I grip is peace on a vice
Accepting my present is truly divine

Naked & Rough Skin

Please don't breathe on me with ease
Coz I'm gonna freeze your breeze with my heat

You seem to see me as if I'm a treat
But I'm here to trick your deeds with chills of my screams

You can't hit me with crazy speed in this scene
I'm already bleeding ink while I stand here on my feet

Just don't bleach me with your preaching
Coz then I'll breach you with my beast & reel you for real

Can you see I'm tearing your sheets in pieces?
It's to reveal the beautiful being on your fluid screen

Can you feel I'm breaking meaningless labels so weak?
It's to fill the space with nothingness from the deep

Can you listen to the beats of this raw sea?
It's just me burning freely my naked & rough skin

Flow *(A collaboration with Grace Hakopian)*

If you see my face
I'd smile in the space
Would you see the real me?
Either way, I'll be free
If you deal with my phase
I'd fall in your gaze
Would you then be afraid?
I'm more than reflection's shade
If you read my phrase
I'd still be traveling my maze
Would you frame what I feel?
I am me, always real
If you stitch with colorful threads
Wound tight, my love still spreads
Would the patterns be revealed?
I'll be courageous, take down my shield
If you look in darker clouds
I stand apart from the crowds
Would you shine the pure energy?
I am my own galactic synergy
If you sea me dead
I still exist, never fled
Would I fly in the sky consciously?
I'd be at home, honestly
If you smell the essence
I'd absorb love's fluorescence
Would you inhale the serenity?
I'd exhale fear's identity
If you sense with grace
I dream the rest of this chase
Would you be divine synchronicity?
I am infinity's electricity

Grace Hakopian

Grace Hakopian is a fearless and free soul. Through her fierce passion of tennis, she found the Universe within her. In many synchronistic dreaming adventures, Grace connected to the awakening within her being. Collaborating with Grace was a pure blessing and a true honour. Just like the title of the poem – **Flow**, there was a natural flow & synchronicity in writing this profound piece with her.

To learn more about Grace and her work, go to:
fearlessfreesoul.com

This is not a final goodbye
Coz energies can never die
The light is shining my eyes
The dark is grounding my sighs
*You'll see me with the ink of my he***art**

Lightning Source UK Ltd.
Milton Keynes UK
UKHW011041231121
394456UK00011B/933